Autism to
An illustrated al

KATHLEEN SHEARER

ISBN: 9781099448102

To mum - Tony's Granny Dot.
Thanks for your patience, kindness and love.

No xylophones or zebras appear in this book

Each letter has a story or thought attached which has emerged unforced and is entirely honest in it's telling. Nothing has been shoe-horned or twisted to fit the A-Z format. Sometimes weeks would pass by before the next picture emerged. So this book has taken quite a while to illustrate and write.

It has felt good to see people laugh in recognition or nod in agreement when I shared pictures and stories with them, perhaps because of their own observations or recollections. These are people who know Tony well. It is my hope that this little book also has a broader appeal. That other people who know and love someone with autism can maybe identify and recognise something in a general sense if not in the specifics.

It is a timely publication. Tony is now approaching his teenage years, so this feels like a celebration of his childhood. It's not always been an easy journey, but it has most certainly been an interesting one!

Kathleen Shearer (aka "Tony's Mum")
June 2019

Autism

I'm using an A-Z of images to help me write about my son and our interesting journey together. I'm hoping to show that autism is part of him, but doesn't define him. You might know a lot about autism but know very little about Tony. If you get to know Tony you might learn a little about autism.

Blanket

The ultimate portable sensory-filter: a blanket. Tony will often lie down or sit with a blanket over his head - we can't see him, but he can still see us through the fibres.

Curiosity

The washing machine: a more immersive sensory experience than watching TV.

Digestives

Friends and family all have some memory of the digestive biscuit phase. Every trip to the supermarket required buying at least one packet of McVities Digestives (no own-brands thank-you-very-much!) The biscuit packet would *not* be opened - rather it was placed with reverence in a very particular place: the radiator; the bathroom sink; a window sill; the mantelpiece; the front door. We all ended up with more digestives than we could possibly eat.

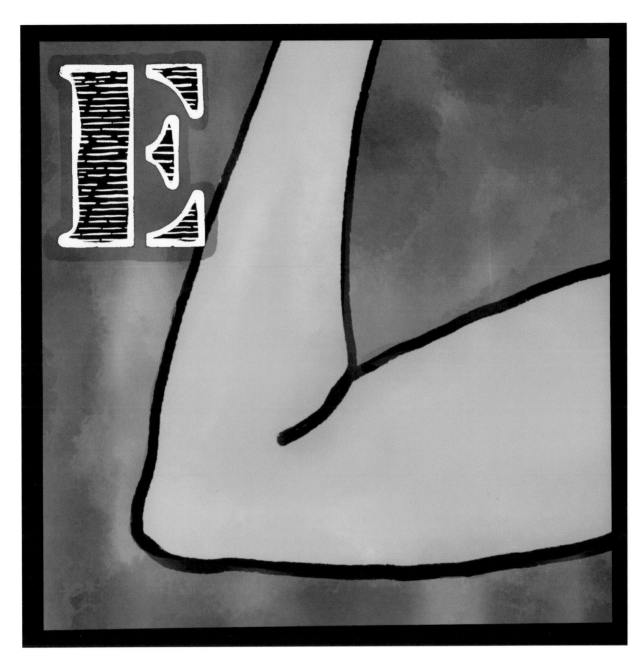

Elbows

Tony helps me appreciate everyday things like elbows. With the gaze of an expert he would examine my elbow from every angle. He would inspect friends and family too. I remember one very patient family (complete strangers) in WH Smiths standing in a line, sleeves rolled up, allowing him to do elbow examinations. For a boy who can't talk, Tony can be very persuasive. And when you think about it - how would we manage *without* elbows? We wouldn't be able to bend our arms. Elbows are wonderfully designed.

Furniture

"So," asks the health professional, "What's Tony really into? Lego? Minecraft? Disney? Cartoons?"
We sit in thoughtful silence...after a while, my mum tentatively says "Moving furniture?". Yes, yes we
all nod in agreement. He likes to move furniture about.

Gloves

Gloves - namely, Marigold Gloves. Yellow is okay, bright fuchsia pink is even better. They turn up in the most unexpected places... like the flower beds in the garden.

Hairstyling

Tony likes to mess up and style people's hair. This happens to me. A lot.

iPad

Tony often won't use things for their intended purpose. So when it comes to technology you have to let him approach it on his terms. I left an iPad lying around the house and he started looking at photos on it, then using the photos to ask things. He is non-verbal so this was a massive step.

He now explores the iPad more. I'm fairly sure he thought "What else does it do that I'm not meant to find out about?" It's good to see him discovering games and puzzles, creating music, finding the volume button and generally having fun. He still uses the photos to communicate.

Jelly Babies

Forget about chocolate. Jelly Babies are better. Probably Tony's favourite sweet. Even at Easter we bought Jelly Bunnies instead of a chocolate egg.

Keys

Tony knows that keys open up doors, sheds, cupboards, cars and all manner of places we probably would rather he didn't go. The key rack and key hooks get placed higher and higher as he grows and stretches. Meanwhile I ponder what I should do when he's taller than me?

Leapfrog toy

Specifically the Leapfrog toy from 2009 which never seemed to run out of batteries and survived being thrown about, trashed and left outside . Then it got lost in a house move and was forgotten about. Until Tony pointed it out as a tiny detail in a photograph. He wanted the Leapfrog toy again.

We couldn't get the current version because they'd updated it beyond all recognition, so we hunted on eBay for the older model. In the end, we bought two (one as a backup). Smart thinking - then he discovered the spare...and we had noisy Leapfrog toys in syncopated stereo.

Music
Tony will often hold a speaker close to his ear. Music brings such joy.

Novelty

We are visiting family friends. "Oh, we made sure and bought plenty of Diet Coke for Tony." Yet we all know which can of juice he will choose. There's nothing Tony likes more than sheer novelty.

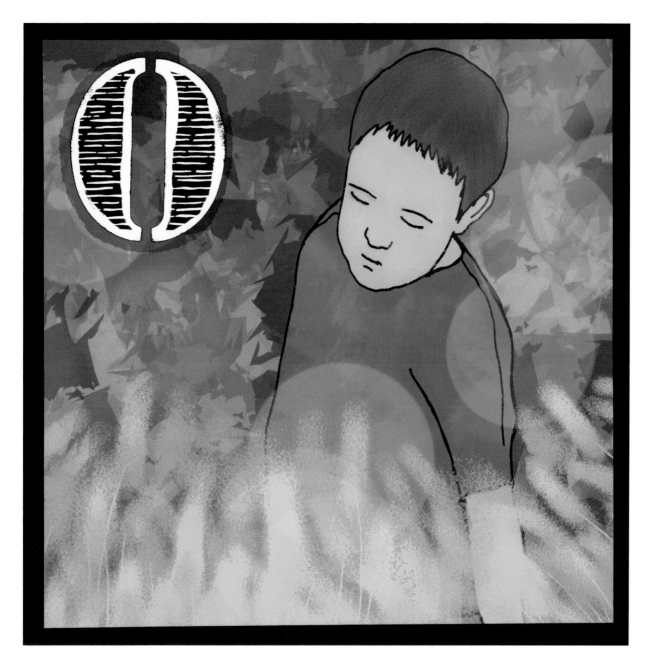

Outdoors

Tony loves being outdoors. He reminds me of the Beatles song "Mother Nature's Son". Picking daisies and leaves, feeling the grass beneath his feet, humming a wordless lazy song beneath the sun. When he is outdoors he is often calmer and seems almost at one with nature.

Pink

I don't know if the colour has a particular visual resonance or if it looks especially appealing, but Tony is drawn towards the colour pink. And it's not just toys - it's washing up liquid, deodorants, marigold gloves (see the letter "G"), ornaments, balloons, juice, wrapping paper and so on. If I want to keep a lunch bag or a water bottle for my own use, I know the last colour I should choose is pink.

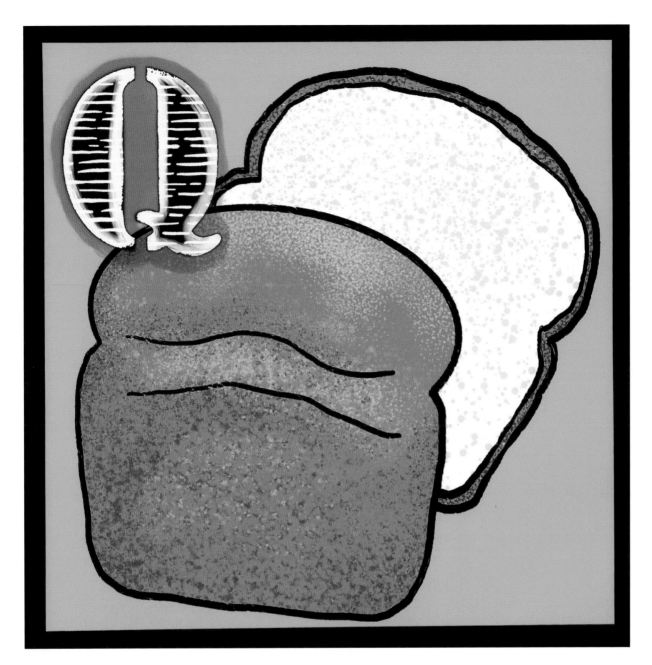

Quirks

Tony doesn't like the heel of the loaf. He never chooses to eat it even though he likes eating crusts and enjoys crusty bread. He won't be tricked either - he checks buttered toast, turning it over to make sure. He also knows if the end of the loaf has been trimmed with a bread knife in a parent's futile attempt to make it look like an ordinary slice. This is but one quirk of his - there are many many more.

Rise Against

Tony's favourite band is Rise Against. They are an American "protest band" but I think others might describe them as "American Punk". I remember a health professional once asking about bedtime routines to help him sleep. "Oh he likes music does he? Something soothing and relaxing maybe?". "Hmmm. Not exactly," I replied, "There's Rise Against (I played a clip from *Revolutions Per Minute*) and Scottish Pipe Bands!"

Sheds

Whether it's the shed at the bottom of the garden; an old rickety locked-up shed or the many on display at the garden centre...you never know quite what you might find in a shed. An unexplored shed is irresistible to Tony.

Trampoline
The boy who has such energy, balance and bounce he could trampoline for Scotland.

Upside down
Quite often, Tony has a different way of looking at things.

Vacuum Cleaners

When Tony was very young, he was scared of the vacuum cleaner. Aged 3 or 4 years old this fear turned to excitement - he would get very animated if he heard or seen a vacuum cleaner. We had a Henry Hoover at the time...and to his fascination, it's slightly sinister smiley face turned up at the school; the shops; public places; and other people's houses.

Weather

When you find yourself googling "barometric pressure and autism" because your child was upset and pointing at a clear blue sky on a sunny day. Only for it to cloud over with a freak snow shower only 20 minutes later. Tony is very sensitive to transitions and changes in the weather.

X-ray

Tony sometimes proves me wrong. "Okay," I say to the dentist, "I'll take him to the hospital for the X-Ray. But there's no way he's going to stand stock still for a whole minute." Which of course is exactly what he did. He was a real superstar that day.

The "Y-factor"

Oxford English Dictionary definition of "y": The second unknown quantity in an algebraic expression, usually the dependent variable.

Where x=the clocks going forward for British Summer Time y=Tony putting the clocks back again. Poor granny got up at 5:00am three days in a row before we figured that one out!

Zzz

Reaching the end of this A-Z feels a bit like when Tony finally switches off and goes to sleep. It's been busy, some moments humdrum and ordinary, others more surprising and eventful. But time to rest now. Tomorrow is another day.

Printed in Great Britain
by Amazon